The (Absolute) Worthlessness of Worry!

Steve Eden

DEDICATION

I am dedicating this book to my incredible wife Stacy, who has grown in intimacy with Jesus so much the last couple of years. She is a beautiful person and smarter than she thinks she is! I Love You Stacy!

CONTENTS

Chapter One
Why We Worry...

My prayer as you read this book is that you allow the Holy Spirit to evict all fear, worry, and anxiety out of your system and set you securely in your true identity as a child of God and disciple (learner/student) of Jesus Christ. I pray you discover your loving Father and Creator never fashioned you for doubt and unbelief but for faith and trust in His unwavering love and goodness!

No matter how far along someone is in Christ, we all feel the pressures of living life in the 21st century. Whether it's raising kids in the lion's den of today's culture and media, conducting business in the current economy, fighting off health issues, or just attempting to juggle family and school and sports where they apply to us - there's a certain weight that comes with just doing life these days.

When your heart gets frequently overwhelmed with the pressures of life, it creates anxiety and worry that can't be ignored. Look no further than the money being made by pharmaceutical companies and the scores of people who are concerned about their stress levels in this nation.

<u>I believe our Heavenly Father wants us to do more than cope with anxiety, I believe He wants us to conquer it.</u> In order to do that we must discover the roots of any fear, worry, and stress, and overcome them with the peace and power of God's Spirit and God's Word.

Why Do We Worry?

The easy answer to this question is we place too much emphasis on us and not enough on God. Of course, there is always the fear factor where we worry because we're afraid of something bad happening. It compounds when we worry about what that bad event happening says about us. When our child acts up in public for example, we often consider, "Oh no, what will others think of me? They're going to think I'm a bad parent, or even worse, a bad person."

Another reason we worry is we lose sight of trusting God for our daily lives, needs, and concerns. We start thinking we are totally on our own through what we *see and feel* around us! It's a scary place to be your only provider and protector with no backing from anyone or anywhere else. Yet, as a born again child of God, you *know* God is with you and *will car*e for you. You have promise after promise in scripture you can stand on, including:

2 Corinthians 9:8 (NLT) – And God will generously provide all you need. Then you will always have everything you need and plenty left over to share with others.

Psalm 23:1 (TPT) – The Lord is my best Friend and my Shepherd, I always have more than enough.

Philippians 4:19 – And my God shall supply all your need according to His riches in glory by Christ Jesus.

Another cause of worry is when we feel if *we don't do something*, nothing will get done right. As a result, we enter into the turmoil of control issues. We want things done *our way,* and because we have little faith in God or in people, we start trying to micromanage everyone and everything. There are many valid reasons why we worry, but Jesus simplifies it even more.

Jesus ties worry to not understanding how much our Heavenly Father values us!

As we look deep into Matthew 6:25-34, pay special attention to Jesus' emphasis on our value to God in verse 26, and God's care for us in verse 30. These are His antidotes for our anxieties.

In Matthew 6:25-34 (NLT) Jesus says, "I tell you not to worry about everyday life— whether you have enough food and drink, or enough clothes to wear. Isn't life more than food, and your body more than clothing? 26 Look at the birds. They don't plant or harvest or store food in barns, yet your heavenly Father feeds them. And aren't you far more valuable to him than they are? 27 Can all your worries add a single moment to your life? 28 "And why worry about your clothing? Look at the lilies of the field and how they grow. They don't work or make clothing, 29 yet Solomon in

4

all his glory was not dressed as beautifully as they are. [30] And if God so cares for wildflowers that are here today and thrown into the fire tomorrow, he will certainly care for you. Why do you have so little faith? [31] "So don't worry about these things, saying, 'What will we eat? What will we drink? What will we wear?' [32] These things dominate the thoughts of unbelievers, but your heavenly Father already knows all your needs. [33] Seek the Kingdom of God above all else, and His righteousness, and he will give you everything you need. [34] "So don't worry about tomorrow, for tomorrow will bring its own worries. Today's trouble is enough for today."

What joy! Jesus says we can *quit trying to quit worrying* and actually invest our time in knowing how much God loves and cares about us! Instead of fighting the darkness of worry, just turn on the light of God's love for you! It is an eternal no contest when darkness meets light!

Think of all the doctors Jesus just helped! They prescribe medication to help those with worry and anxiety, yet now they can also point people to a tried and true medication for worry – knowing how much they're valued by Almighty

God! When worry comes knocking, we can return to that famous little song that carries so much power, "Jesus loves me this I know, for the Bible tells me so!"

Jesus ties God's protection and provision for our daily lives not to our performance, but to how much we matter to the Father! So instead of trying to get big faith, get a big grasp on God's love! Get to know your Heavenly Father, because to know Him is to trust Him, and to trust Him is to defeat all worry.

Chapter Two
The Worthlessness Of Worry

In Matthew 6:27 (NIV) Jesus says, "Can any one of you by worrying add a single hour to your life?"

Jesus points out in this passage the absolute worthlessness of worry. He is literally asking us to consider, "What good is worry?"

One day the Lord dropped into my heart this statement, "Steve, worry is worthless because it's unnecessary, unfruitful, unnatural, and undermines your value to God." I was taken back and immediately desired to search out all He could mean! I began sitting with Him and digging into Scripture and here is what I found:

1. Worry Is Unnecessary

Worry is unnecessary because it doesn't affect or change one single outcome or circumstance for the good. Can worrying about your child's first day of school, for example, change how their day

7

goes? Can worrying about a school bully keep them from picking on your child? Can worrying over your finances cause your bank account to grow? Your time is better spent sitting with the Lord and asking for wisdom and a plan; rather than worrying, fretting, and pondering doomsday outcomes.

Worry is unnecessary because it doesn't add to you, strengthen you, increase your wisdom, or build your faith in any way. On the contrary, it takes dead aim at your health and peace of mind. American doctors mention frequently the destructive role of worry and anxiety in heart disease and how they can take years off of your life. When Jesus said worry doesn't ADD to your life, He is confirming this medical fact.

<u>Worry is a thief and a trespasser on the heart and mind of any child of God! Worry robs people of their health, steals their peace of mind, and snatches their Christ-like attitudes.</u>

Jesus said in John 10:10, "The thief comes only to steal, kill, and destroy, but I have come that you might have life and have it more abundantly."

So many times the worry we are housing is worse for us than whatever it is we are worrying about. When the Covid19 pandemic alert came out, I continued to remind the body of Christ that all the worry, fear, and anxiety coming from the media and the Internet is every bit as harmful as Covid19!

You Become Like What You Behold

It is a law of life that you become like that which you behold. So, if all you behold is negative news, fearful scenarios, and confusion, worry is gonna get on you and in you. It was stunning how many Americans and yes, even Christ-filled Americans, glued themselves to their televisions and mobile devices for the latest download of death and fear from a secular news media that was not capable of delivering any Godly or faith-filled perspective about Covid19.

2 Corinthians 3:18, however, says we can behold the glory of the Lord and be transformed into His image. Here is the entire verse:

But we all, with unveiled face, beholding as in a mirror the glory of the Lord, are being transformed into the same image from glory to glory, just as by the Spirit of the Lord.

If you're beholding God's glory consistently, you'll be transformed into His image and likeness! This is good news considering our Heavenly Father is never full of tormenting fear, worry, or anxiety! Those things can't fill a heart that's already filled with the Lord's glory and perspective so fix your eyes on Him.

Bottom line is, whatever has your attention has you, so don't let the enemy use worry to keep your attention off the Lord, where it should be.

2. Worry Is Unfruitful

Worry is unfruitful because Jesus said in Matthew 13:22 it "chokes the Word" at work in the soil of your heart, and doesn't allow you to bring forth His fruit. Jesus desires we reflect Him and His Spirit each and every day, even in the face of test or trial. The beautifying fruit of love, joy, peace, patience, kindness, and goodness find it hard to be expressed when the ugliness of worry is lurking around.

In Matthew 13:22 (NIV) Jesus says "The seed falling among the thorns refers to someone who hears the word, but the worries of this life and the deceitfulness of wealth choke the word, making it unfruitful."

Not only does worry try to nullify the fruit of Christ's Spirit, the fruit we produce at the hands of worry are medical calamities such as anxiety, anger, stress, panic, speculation, paranoia, and yes, heart disease. [1]Researchers found that anxiety was associated with a 26% increased risk of coronary heart disease and a 48% increased risk of heart related death! And why wouldn't it be? Worry is mediating on a lie. A lie that God isn't enough for us and our situation.

While it is true that our own ideas and limited thinking might not be enough, God and His worry-free Spirit, along with the mind of Christ living inside of us are more than enough!

1 Corinthians 2:9-12 and verse 16 (ESV) says, "But, as it is written, "No eye has seen, nor ear heard, nor the heart of man imagined, what God has prepared for those who love him"—

11

[10] but these things God has revealed to us through the Spirit. For the Spirit searches everything, even the depths of God. [11] For who knows a person's thoughts except the spirit of that person, which is in him? So also no one comprehends the thoughts of God except the Spirit of God. [12] Now we have received not the spirit of the world, but the Spirit who is from God, that we might understand the things freely given us by God.... [16] For who has understood the mind of the Lord so as to instruct him?" But we have the mind of Christ."

This passage is one of my favorites because it points out the resources we have at our access in Christ: His Holy Spirit and His mind! A revolutionary truth of Christianity is that Jesus died for us that He might live *in us!* Our lives are now able to be lived in *union* with Him. We can know His thoughts and perspectives.

Think of the human mind as a computer, worrisome thoughts as a virus, and the Holy Spirit within us as anti-virus software that has been downloaded to our hard drive. Once the Holy Spirit has been introduced to us, we can

access Him and our new mind in Christ in order
to drive out all anxious thoughts.

Verse 11 communicates, "No one knows the
thoughts of God but the Spirit of God." So many
times I've faced a tough decision. So many times
I've wasted hours trying to come up with a full
proof plan of my own only to hear the Holy Spirit
say, "The answer you're looking for is in Me, not
in the wisdom of natural man."

What joy to know that when we don't know what
to do about a challenging relationship or tragic
circumstance, we have the mind of Christ within
us and God's Spirit to show us the way!

3. Worry Is Unnatural

Worry is unnatural because your body, soul, and
spirit are all designed for faith not for fear. We
thrive and live much healthier lives in faith,
peace, rest, and trust than in fear and suspicion.
Always keep in mind that you are never at your
best in fear or worry.

Every life attitude Jesus taught and modeled is
life giving and health producing for human

beings. Love, joy, peace and on and on it goes –
they all foster health! He and His Spirit are not
just the way to Heaven, they are the way we are
designed to live!

[1]In the USA, anxiety disorders are the most
common type of mental illness, affecting 40
million adults, or 18% of the population. Clearly
worry, fear, and anxiety are not the natural
emotions God designed us to plug into.

Here's two translations of Ecclesiastes 11:10:

**Ecclesiastes 11:10 (NLT) – So refuse to worry
and keep your body healthy...**

**Ecclesiastes 11:10 (NIV) – So then, banish
anxiety from your heart and cast off the
troubles of your body...**

Why are worry and anxiety unhealthy and
troublesome to your body? Because they are
unnatural to you. They do not *fit you* because of
the law of creation and design. You are created
in the image of God, and being made in His
image, you aren't designed for worry.

Notice you are to *banish* worry from *your heart* because that's where the enemy likes to grow his seeds of despair and destruction. God, on the other hand, wants to grow His seeds of truth and love in your heart, producing in you His Life which is completely natural and native for you.

4. Worry Undermines Your Value

Lastly, I want to remind you how Jesus told His disciples in Matthew 6:25-26 (TLB) that worry is present in their lives because they don't understand how much their Heavenly Father values them. Here's the two verses:

"So my counsel is: Don't worry about *things*— food, drink, and clothes. For you already have life and a body—and they are far more important than what to eat and wear. [26] Look at the birds! They don't worry about what to eat—they don't need to sow or reap or store up food—for your heavenly Father feeds them. <u>And you are far more valuable to him than they are</u>."

Not knowing our Father as the source of our value and esteem is incredibly problematic.

15

Without fail, when sourced by and identified by anything other than God's Spirit, we become susceptible to seeking our worth from people and things which will produce great instability as well as insecurity.

Having God As Your Source

So many of us have simply and erroneously looked for how much we matter in everything but God. How many parents are up and down emotionally with their children's grades? How many adults are up and down with how much money they make? How many teens are up and down by how many friends they have? It is easy to do. Thankfully, there is hope!

Any time you are feeling less than, devalued, insignificant, or your attitudes and emotions are on the negative side instead of the Christ-like side, ask yourself this question. "Who or what is the source of my frustration right now?" Then as the Holy Spirit reveals His perspective of where you're off track and what you should do next - OBEY HIM.

If you want stability, identity, and security each day, always make sure your Heavenly Father, not the behavior of others or your circumstances, is your source!

When you're manifesting the fruit of Christ's Spirit from Galatians 5:22-23, then you know you're being sourced by Him. As a result, even if your child's grades are lower than you'd like, you're not living and dying with what all that says about you, your value, or your child's value.

This discipline to assess yourself will also help you when your child's grades *are good* and you start deriving all your identity from how smart they must be *because of you!* It's certainly ok to feel a measure of joy that your child is doing well in school, but your primary source must always be your Heavenly Father and who He says you are.

This principle of being properly sourced is why God told Jesus on the front end of His ministry that He was His beloved Son and that He was well pleased with Him. (Luke 3:21-22)

As a result of His Father's declaration, everything Jesus did in ministry was never chasing value or seeking His Father's approval, but rather from a place of safety, security, identity, and acceptance.

Maybe you don't have a worry problem, maybe you are connected to the wrong source, or maybe you simply lack faith in how much your Father loves and values you! Whatever the root, invite Jesus to expose it, expel it, and empower you to walk out your continued freedom and obedience!

Chapter Three
Rediscovering the Love Of God

Prayerfully, you've begun to notice having a firsthand experiential knowledge of God's love is crucial to overcoming fear, worry, and anxiety. According to Paul in Ephesians chapter 3, being rooted and grounded in our Father's love is of the utmost importance to living both a full and fulfilled life.

Ephesians 3:14-19 says, "For this reason I bow my knees to the Father of our Lord Jesus Christ, [15] from whom the whole family in heaven and earth is named, [16] that He would grant you, according to the riches of His glory, to be strengthened with might through His Spirit in the inner man, [17] that Christ may dwell in your hearts through faith; that you, being rooted and grounded in love, [18] may be able to comprehend with all the saints what is the width and length and depth and height—

¹⁹ to know the love of Christ which passes knowledge; that you may be filled with all the fullness of God."

What an incredible prayer! The apostle Paul, rightfully and needfully so, prays that each and every saint wholeheartedly and experientially knows how wide, long, deep, and high our Father's love truly is! Paul desires we live rooted and grounded in God's relentless love for us!

God won't make you love Him, but you don't have the power to make Him not love you. The sooner you grasp the eternal duration of His love, the sooner you can consistently defeat enemies like fear and worry. I admonish you by the Spirit of Christ Himself to sit with the Lord by taking time with Him and the scripture daily and purpose to rediscover His amazing love!

Scripture doesn't say God *has* love for you, it says God IS LOVE! If He just *has* love for you, it could be measured and could run out. But, He is love, therefore, His loving you is tied to His character and infallible nature. He would cease being God if He stopped loving you!

Looking Unto Jesus

Jesus faced enormous challenges and pressures in His life, yet He took on everything without giving place to fear or worry. For example, real pressure is when your mother asks you to perform a miracle before it is your time to be revealed as the Messiah. Pressure is when your friends ask you to keep a man from dying but you can't get there on time because people are trying to assassinate you. Pressure is when you're always being falsely accused and slandered over things you didn't do. Lastly, pressure is when you're in a garden interceding for world transformation and your disciples are asleep!

So why didn't Jesus succumb to the fear, strain, and anxiety many of us would have succumbed to in similar circumstances? Did He *have* something you and I don't? No, but He KNEW something you and I often don't. He knew how much His Father loved Him. He was rooted and grounded and commissioned in His Father's love.

You see, in Luke 3:21-22, the Father had opened the heavens and spoke to Jesus, "You are My beloved Son, in You I am well pleased." God

21

speaks this to Him BEFORE He has done any miracles or ministry! Jesus knew no fear or anxiety because He knew His Father had sent Him, identified Him, loved Him, qualified Him, and most of all was present with Him to perform His Word.

In John 8:28-29 Jesus says, "When you lift up the Son of Man, then you will know that I am He, and that I do nothing of Myself; but as My Father taught Me, I speak these things. [29] <u>And He who sent Me is with Me. The Father has not left Me alone, for I always do those things that please Him.</u>"

Notice how secure Jesus was in His Father's Presence and purpose. Have you discovered that you too are here on God's behalf and for His purpose? Are you fully convinced the Father who sent you is with you? That you are here to advance His Kingdom, not build, save, or keep your own? When you surrender to the Father's purpose and Presence, you (like Jesus), can have full confidence that all of Heaven backs you and you have nothing to fear. You are kept by your Heavenly Father, loved by Him, and on mission with Him!

God's Revelation of Himself

1 John 4:17-18 says, "Love has been perfected among us in this: that we may have boldness in the day of judgment; because as He is, so are we in this world. [18] <u>There is no fear in love; but perfect love casts out fear, because fear involves torment. But he who fears (torment) has not been made perfect in love.</u>"

While there is a *healthy* fear of the Lord, many are bound by an *unhealthy* fear of Him. A healthy fear of the Lord is to respect Him, and to hold Him in highest honor. An unhealthy fear of the Lord is to believe He is a tyrant who is anything but loving, kind, compassionate, or understanding. John is saying in verse 18, if you're struggling with fear that involves torment and punishment, you've not understood nor matured in God's perfect love for you.

I truly believe there are still many well-meaning believers who are absolutely convinced God is ready to bring the hammer down on them if they don't perform adequately. This creates many issues. It is difficult at best to have a close relationship with a God you believe will leave you when you disappoint Him or make a mistake. It is quite challenging to be intimate with a God you believe is applying immense pressure upon you to perform. It is straight up impossible to put the whole weight of your being and full trust in a God you believe is not approachable and doesn't really love you! When you're in a place of not being able to fully trust God, you become an easy target for fear and worry!

Thankfully, Jesus Christ came to reveal the true nature of our Heavenly Father; which is to save us not destroy us, to love us not harm us, and to bring us near to Himself! Then, once He brought us near, to never leave us nor forsake us. This gives us the stability we need to know Him, to trust Him, and to live abundant lives in today's culture that's rife with opportunities for anxiety.

In John 14:9 Jesus said, "If you've seen Me, you've seen your Father." I believe Jesus is saying here, I know you have questions about how Almighty God really feels about you and who He really is, but I came to reveal the answers you need. Instead of killing all of His enemies, God through His Son reconciled the world to

Himself by giving His life for them. This is an endearing love that casts out all fear.

Romans 5:8 verifies this, saying, "But God demonstrates His own love toward us, in that while we were still sinners, Christ died for us."

2 Corinthians 5:18-19 adds, "Now all things are of God, who has reconciled us to Himself through Jesus Christ, and has given us the ministry of reconciliation, [19] that is, that God was in Christ reconciling the world to Himself, not imputing their trespasses to them, and has committed to us the word of reconciliation."

What makes Jesus' revelation of God the Father so amazing is that He is not some man's revelation of God, He is God's very revelation of Himself! According to verse 19, God was where? God was *in Christ*, reconciling the world to Himself! You *can trust* God's perfect and personal revelation of Himself!

In John 10:30, Jesus says, "The Father and I are one."

John 1:18 (AMPC) says, "No man has ever seen God at any time; but the only unique Son, or the only begotten God, Who is in the bosom [in the intimate presence] of the Father, He has declared Him [He has revealed Him and brought Him out where He can be seen; He has interpreted Him and made Him known]."

Jesus Christ is not man become God but God become man. He is not man reaching upward, He is God reaching downward. We could not get to God, so God came to us in human form. He came to us in a body we could relate to. He came to us speaking a language we could actually understand. Jesus reveals that God's love for us is infinitely personal. Not only did we see the face of our Father through the face of the Son, we were touched by the Father's hands through Jesus and heard our Father's voice through Him. Jesus is God saying to you, I'm not aloof. I'm not impersonal. I'm right here. I am with you and for you. Jesus Christ is Emmanuel, God is with us, sent to cast out all invading fear. Thus, the revelation that God is Christ-like remains one of the most important revelations every Christ follower should pursue and receive!

The Revelation Is Personal

In Matthew 11:28 Jesus said, "Come unto Me." He did not say come unto My religion. He did not say come unto My teaching. He did not say come unto My philosophy. He did not say come unto My book. He said come unto Me! This is such an incredibly personal invitation to relationship.

There are many religions but only one gospel! Religion is man's search for God but the gospel is God's search for man! This means if you are lost you do not have to find Him, He will find you. And when He does, just turn around and you are immediately in the arms of redemptive love.

Why didn't God remain distant and just reveal himself to us in nature or creation? I mean - the sky, the moon, the stars, the rivers are all beautiful, God could have just used them. It's because they are too impersonal and too inconsistent to reveal Him. A river could carry a boy down stream to his dad or a river could be a place where a young boy drowns. God wanted to make sure you knew He was not neutral towards you, but rather He is for you and can be relied upon, so He came personally in His Son.

Romans 8:31-39 verifies this in saying, "What then shall we say to these things? If God is for us, who can be against us? [32] He who did not spare His own Son, but delivered Him up for us all, how shall He not with Him also freely give us all things? [33] Who shall bring a charge against God's elect? It is God who justifies. [34] Who is he who condemns? It is Christ who died, and furthermore is also risen, who is even at the right hand of God, who also makes intercession for us. [35] Who shall separate us from the love of Christ? Shall tribulation, or distress, or persecution, or famine, or nakedness, or peril, or sword? [36] As it is written: "For Your sake we are killed all day long; we are accounted as sheep for the slaughter." [37] Yet in all these things we are more than conquerors through Him who loved us. [38] For I am persuaded that neither death nor life, nor angels nor principalities nor powers, nor things present nor things to come, [39] nor height nor depth, nor any other created thing, shall be able to separate us from the love of God which is in Christ Jesus our Lord."

This is one of my favorite passages in all the Bible because Paul is saying, God is not the one condemning you or bringing your charges before the judge, He's the One who justified you and paid the price to set you free! He's not only incredibly good and generous; He's for you, He's personal, and He's approachable!

My Testimony

I can honestly say that my own personal encounter with my Heavenly Father's agape love changed the trajectory of my life forever and gave me the security I needed to face life's challenges. Do I still worry from time to time? Sure, but now I have the foundation of His love to defeat it when it comes knocking!

My whole world changed the day I discovered God loves me because He's so good not because I'm always so good. I became free the day I actually knew and believed He loved me not because I'm so pure but because He's so pure.

When I was 20 years old and playing college baseball at Northeastern State University in Tahlequah, Oklahoma, I had a personal encounter with Christ. I had asked Jesus into my heart at age 13, but spent the next 7 years trying to earn His acceptance and love. Thankfully, in college, by His grace, He allowed me to experience His loving Presence, His truth, and His Voice in a very tangible way!

I had one particular sin/weakness that I really struggled with. After faltering over and over in my daily attempts to overcome it, I felt like a total failure as a Christian. So, as was my routine, one day I was begging for God's forgiveness. I was accustomed to telling God what a lousy person I was, and so for what seemed like the 500th time, I told Him I was sorry for the sin that had a hold on me. Of course, the enemy was laying a lot of shame and guilt on me. I felt like I was getting nowhere. Then suddenly, the Spirit of the Lord Jesus Christ came lovingly into my room, stood in front of me, and overwhelmed me with His grace. I cried and cried because I felt so unworthy of Him and His love for me. I literally asked Him, "How can *You* love someone like *me*?"

He said, "Steve, because you are Mine to love. I purchased you with My blood and I am incapable of leaving you or forsaking you. I bought you with a price. You belong to Me." He added, "I do not love you because of what you do; I love you because of who I am. So when you walk out of this room today, I want you to live the rest of your life FROM My love and not FOR it. The truth is - nothing you ever do or don't do will change My eternal love for you."

As you might imagine, this powerful and very real encounter had a profound affect on me as a person and certainly as a Christ follower. I suddenly began to realize all my attempts at getting God to love me were rooted in unbelief and not faith! His perfect love came and began casting out all my fears and torments! Fear of not being enough. Fear of being rejected and not being accepted. Fear of needing to be in control. I was learning to be safe in His agape love. I'm still learning to walk out my freedom in these areas, but what a beginning and foundation!

Learning and growing in God's love is very much my prayer for you! But it must be yours and it must be personal between *you* and the Lord.

The (Absolute) Worthlessness of Worry!

Chapter Four
Knowing And Believing God's Love

1 John 4:16 says, "And we have <u>known and</u> <u>believed</u> the love that God has for us. God is love, and he who abides in love abides in God, and God in him."

I like how the apostle John notes the importance of both knowing (a personal experience with), and believing (an acting upon our personal experience with), the love of God. We must know *AND* believe the love God has for us in order to live a victorious life over the worry, stress, and strain of this world.

<u>Despite your less than perfect track record, God's</u> <u>perfect love for you has never wavered. His love</u> <u>for you will not and cannot fail. You must know</u> <u>*AND* believe His love is based on the character of</u> <u>the Giver not the conduct of the receiver.</u>

Only then can you begin to have a strong sense of safety, security, and comfort that no matter what you face, HE is with you! Knowing *AND* believing God's love for you empowers you into a daily, intra-personal, intimate relationship with Him!

Knowing *AND* believing God's love for you leads you to believe all His other promises are true as well. For example, living in the reality of God's love allows you to believe God *really has* forgiven you of all your sin - past, present, and future. It also empowers you to accept all His promises of provision and protection are true!

It is not enough to just *believe* the good news about God's love though, we must KNOW it by personal experience. That's what brings transformation and quells all fear. Look no further than my testimony I shared in chapter three. It launched me on a *journey* of personally knowing, by experience, the love of Jesus Christ! In reality, my encounter with Jesus in college wasn't the end of me knowing God's love for me, it was the beginning! It seeded in me a great desire to be *growing in my knowing* of my Father's love.

In John 17:3 Jesus says perhaps the most important statement ever uttered, "And this is

eternal life, that they may KNOW you, the only true God, and Jesus Christ whom You have sent."

The word "know" here is Ginosko in the Greek language. Ginosko according to my research on Biblehub and the Strong's Concordance means: To know, especially through personal experience (first hand acquaintance not passed down from another). It means to experientially and intimately know; citing this example from Luke 1:34, "And Mary said to the angel, "How will this be since I do not KNOW a man?"

This definition gives the connotation of an absolute oneness and personal knowing. It's the same Greek Word used in 1 John 4:16 which began this chapter, saying we must *KNOW* and believe the love God has for us!

God desires all of us to be able to confidently say, "I know and believe the love God has for me and now I see my world differently. I see adversity differently. I see fear differently, and I *ACT* differently. I know the worst thing that could happen in adversity or trial is He works it all for my and everyone else's good!"

The Stunning "Chesed" Love Of God

There are a handful of words from scripture that translate to the English word "love." I encourage you to look into them when you have time so that you can grow in your personal knowledge and experience of the love of God. Words such as "agape" love, "phileo" love, and others are worth sitting with the Lord in.

One type of biblical love you simply *must* look into with depth that drives out the insidiousness of fear and worry, is God's *chesed love!* "Chesed" is one of the Hebrew translations for love in the Old Testament.

Hebrew scholars will tell you that God's chesed love is His lovingkindness and mercy as a covenant loyalty towards His people. It has the connotation of the stronger party, God, always leaning into the weaker party, us. Chesed is a life long love that is rooted in a covenant relationship. It is a steadfast faithfulness that endures throughout eternity.

You may have the thought, "OK, but am I in covenant with God since I'm not Jewish? Does His chesed love apply to me?" As a born again Christian, you are in covenant with God through His Son Jesus Christ who now lives in you by the Holy Spirit. Therefore, chesed, God's steadfast love rooted in His covenant loyalty, ABSOLUTELY applies to you! Paul saw this so well he calls you a "Jew inwardly" in Romans 2:29. Hebrews 8 also outlines in detail the reality of the New Covenant that's available through Christ.

Here are several passages in the Old Testament where the Hebrew word "chesed" is found. I have underlined the English translation for you in each passage.

Lamentations 3:22-23 (NLT) says, "The <u>faithful love</u> of the Lord never ends! His mercies never cease. [23] Great is his faithfulness; his mercies begin afresh each morning."

Jeremiah 31:3 testifies, "…Yes, I have loved you with an everlasting love; therefore, with <u>lovingkindness</u> I have drawn you."

In Hosea 2:19-20 God says, "I will betroth you to Me forever; Yes, I will betroth you to Me in righteousness and justice, in <u>lovingkindness</u> and mercy; [20] I will betroth you to Me in faithfulness, and you shall know the Lord."

Psalm 145:8 says, "The Lord is gracious and full of compassion, slow to anger and great in <u>mercy</u>."

Psalm 136 uses the term chesed 26 times and is interpreted this way in these bible translations:

NIV – His *love* endures forever
KJV – His *mercy* endureth forever
ESV – His *steadfast love* endures forever
MSG – His *love* never quits
NLT – His *faithful love* endures forever
NASB – His *lovingkindness* is everlasting

All these are translations of the phrase, "kiy l'olam hesedo," which creates the echoing refrain of Psalm 136.

It is hard to take such a descriptive word like chesed and condense its meanings to one word in the English language. Chesed involves kindness, specifically God's kindness to us, a creature that often comes up short in trying to reflect His image. It involves His mercy as well, born out of His gracious forgiveness toward us. So chesed love is kindness and mercy, but it is more than that. It is love, but it is more than that. It also involves commitment, revealed in the covenant God has made and keeps with us despite our missteps.

When speaking of God it conveys the steady faithfulness He has to his undeserving people, and is descriptive of the One who has done so much to save and shepherd them. We could never remain faithful as He has, nor could we maintain the covenant. But God, with His incredible chesed love, goes beyond what we deserve to show mercy and lavish His love upon us.

Chesed is a form of love that extends beyond any sin or betrayal in order to heal the broken-hearted and to graciously extend forgiveness to them. It is love with no limits or boundaries.

Your Father's love is like the waves of the ocean! Unrelenting! His love just keeps coming and coming no matter the circumstances. His love leans into your brokenness as the stronger and more complete party in the covenant relationship.

Perhaps an old Dennis the Menace cartoon can help us understand more fully! As the cartoon frame begins, Dennis and his friend are walking to Mrs. Wilson's home. In the next frame, the boys come out with arm loads of cookies! The next frame, Dennis' friend asks him a very good question, "Dennis, what do you suppose we did to *deserve* all these cookies?" In the final frame, Dennis responds with an amazing revelation, "I don't think we got all these cookies cuz' we're so good, I think we got them because Mrs. Wilson is so good!"

That, my friends, is how any of us got saved, got good enough for Jesus to die for, or became candidates for the unending, unrelenting, chesed love of God!! This is a love we must know AND believe!

Chesed In the New Testament

The Greek equivalent to chesed love is the word "eleos," which translates to mercy, compassion, covenant love, and covenant loyalty. It is God's readiness to help those in trouble. It is mercy, kindness, and goodwill toward the afflicted; joined with a desire to relieve them of their misery. Here are some examples of eleos in the New Testament I've underlined for you:

Titus 3:4-5 - But when the kindness and the love of God our Savior toward man appeared, [5] not by works of righteousness which we have done, but according to His _mercy_ He saved us, through the washing of regeneration and renewing of the Holy Spirit…

Hebrews 4:16 - Let us therefore come boldly to the throne of grace, that we may obtain _mercy_ and find grace to help in time of need.

Matthew 9:10-13 - Now it happened, as Jesus sat at the table in the house, that behold, many tax collectors and sinners came and sat down with Him and His disciples. [11] And when the Pharisees saw it, they said to His disciples, "Why does your Teacher eat with tax collectors and sinners?" [12] When Jesus heard that, He said to them, "Those who are well have no need of a physician, but those who are

sick. [13] **But go and learn what this means: 'I desire _mercy_ and not sacrifice.' For I did not come to call the righteous, but sinners, to repentance."**

Matthew 12:7 - But if you had known what this means, 'I desire _mercy_ and not sacrifice,' you would not have condemned the guiltless.

Jesus is explaining God has a soft spot for those who stumble but whose hearts are postured towards Him. On the other hand, He gets no satisfaction from people who don't really love Him but keep all the rules they can.

Some Other Thoughts

It used to bother me that the word charity was often used for the word love in the King James translation, so I decided to look up its meaning. I found charity is giving to someone who can't possibly pay you back. Doing for someone who can't do for you. It is giving what is undeserved. Based on these definitions, it's clear charity is a great description of what God's love is really like - both charitable and unconditional. He loves because He's so pure not because we always are.

Titus 1:15 says, "To the pure all things are pure, but to those who are defiled and unbelieving nothing is pure..."

I will never forget the day the Lord took me to this passage and said, "Steve, I didn't give My Life for the world because their hearts were so pure, I gave it because My heart is so pure. Everyone, in My eyes, was worth dying for."

My goodness, let all that truth sink in! Let each of us know *AND* believe the love God has for us!

The (Absolute) Worthlessness of Worry!

Chapter Five
Learning To Rest

According to the American Institute of Stress, Americans are among the most stressed-out populations in the world. Drawing from Gallup's 2019 data on emotions, over half of the American population (55%) experience stress during the day. This is 20% higher than the world average of 35%.

The opposite of stress is rest. Jesus came offering a Godly and peace-filled rest for your soul that will empower you to defeat stress.

If you're born again, you have rest in your spirit man that is never fearful or stressed. Your soul (mind, will, and emotions) and body however, need this same rest that is from Christ to lead and govern them. <u>You need the best of you, your spirit man, to lead the rest of you, your soul and body.</u> Your emotions and thoughts need to be regularly subjected to the Spirit of Christ inside you.

This is often easier said than done though as life in this world can be taxing and trying. You may be wondering, like many others who face adversity, "How do I keep my emotions and thoughts under subjection to Christ?"

Jesus' Rhythm of Grace

In Matthew 11:28-30 (ESV) Jesus says, "Come to me, all you who labor and are heavy burdened, and I will give you rest. [29] Take my yoke upon you, and learn from me, for I am gentle and lowly in heart, and you will find rest for your souls. [30] For my yoke is easy, and my burden is light."

In this passage, Jesus reveals a step by step "Rhythm of Grace" that I believe will lead you and others in resisting stress and embracing the rest God offers! He says:

Come To Me

No matter what is going on in our lives, when we're weary and feeling burdened, Jesus invites us to come to Him first and foremost. Too often we attempt to tackle the stressful events of our day without engaging Him first.

In Matthew 6:33 Jesus says, "Seek first the Kingdom of God and His righteousness, and all these things shall be added to you."

In other words, before you seek all the answers to something, and certainly before you begin stressing over it, come immediately to Jesus, hungering and thirsting for His righteousness to prevail!

Take My Yoke

A yoke is designed so that two can function as *one*. Literally, it's been created so two can share a load together. Two oxen or two horses can be yoked together so they can pull a sled or plow while sharing the weight and resistance of the plow. Jesus wants you sharing life's loads with Him! He even says His yoke is easy and light for us! God didn't make you to carry your sin or the cares of this life. He absolutely did not make you to carry the dysfunction of those around you. Therefore, cleave to Jesus, not to people and their problems! Stay yoked to Jesus not to the drama of this world, and find yourself living *too blessed to be stressed!*

Learn From Me

Regardless of what you may face, Jesus wants to reveal Himself to you in that challenge. He wants to be not only your leader but also your shining example. Jesus was always on. It didn't matter if Judas was stealing from Him or Pilate was interrogating Him, He was never worried or anxious. Let His example and His internal Presence speak to you, settle you, and anchor you.

Hebrews 12:1-3 says, "Therefore we also, since we are surrounded by so great a cloud of witnesses, let us lay aside every weight, and the sin which so easily ensnares us, and let us run with endurance the race that is set before us, [2] looking unto Jesus, the author and finisher of our faith, who for the joy that was set before Him endured the cross, despising the shame, and has sat down at the right hand of the throne of God. [3] For consider Him who endured such hostility from sinners against

Himself, lest you become discouraged and weary in your souls."

I believe the sin that so easily entangles us is when we fix our eyes on other things rather than looking to Jesus! We become like that which we behold so let's behold Him not our adversity. Also, notice by *considering* Jesus' example and learning from Him as verse 3 says, we do not grow weary or lose heart through any trial or tribulation. The fact is, no one has endured more suffering than Jesus, so learn from Him in persevering through all suffering, pain, and persecution.

Find Rest For Your Soul

So coming unto Jesus, taking His yoke, and learning from Him will activate the very Spirit of Christ that's in you and thus produce rest not stress in your soul and body! Rest will bring renewal even if it's in small doses. Rest brings a healthy rhythm back to life and sets us in a place of trusting the Lord in all things rather than needing to control all things.

Isaiah 26:3 says, "You (Lord) will keep him in perfect peace, whose mind is stayed on You, because he trusts in You."

What goes on around us isn't the source of our stress, it's actually how we process and perceive what goes on around us. It's what our mind fixes on and stays on. Your kids, for example, aren't the source of your worry, how you relate to them and perceive their drama is the source of your worry. Rather than letting the devil *stress* you, let God *stretch* you and your faith in the challenges of life.

Chapter Six
Gardening Your Heart

Whatever you allow into your heart will grow. We know this because Jesus likens the human heart to soil that *needs to be tended* in Matthew 13:22. Good gardeners know that good gardens don't just happen, there is time and intentionality invested in its care. Your heart, according to Jesus, can give place to seeds *or* weeds, so it is important that you guard, protect, and *garden* your heart.

No one can tend the soil of your heart for you. You must tend it, understanding the power of your choices and priorities. Just like no one can make you worry, no one can make you garden your heart; you choose!

In Deuteronomy 30:19 God says, "I have set before you life and death, blessing and cursing; therefore choose life..."

Choose to garden your heart by allowing the good seed in and keeping the weeds of worry out. Be receptive to God's truth and be on guard against the enemy's deceptions.

Proverbs 4:20-23 (NLT) says, "My child, pay attention to what I say. Listen carefully to my words. [21] Don't lose sight of them. <u>Let them penetrate deep into your heart,</u> [22] for they bring life to those who find them, and healing to their whole body. [23] <u>Guard your heart above all else, for it determines the course of your life."</u>

According to verse 23, whatever is going on in your heart determines the course of your life! Getting you to receive Christ was easy, but getting you to guard and tend the soil of your heart is a greater challenge. One way you can is through renewing your mind daily.

Romans 12:2 says, "And do not be conformed to this world but be transformed by the renewing of your mind..."

Renewing your mind is an important discipline because just like your eyes and ears are the *gateway* to your mind; your mind is the *gateway* to your heart, and your heart is the soil where things grow!

It is fair to say then, when worrisome thoughts are allowed to stick around in your mind, they eventually take root in your heart producing bad fruit. What is bad fruit? Anything that doesn't look like Christ and His fruit of the Spirit outlined in Galatians 5:22-23. His fruit are things like love, joy, peace, patience, kindness, and self-control. Good seed plus good soil always equals good fruit!

If we are not careful and intentional about renewing our mind, our heart can quickly be cluttered with negative thoughts that take root. When adversity comes, if worry and anxiety get into your heart and get rooted, they stress your heart, mind, and body. Once you are vexed by stress, it can begin to negatively influence those around you and the atmosphere of your home, family, and marriage.

The Power Of Your Mind

My pastor, Duane Sheriff, often says, "The power of the Christian life does not come *from* the mind, but it does come *through* the mind."

Nowhere in the Bible are we commanded to fix our minds on all our problems. However, we are asked to renew our mind, set our mind, think on whatever is true, be of the same mind as Christ, be of sound mind, and be renewed in the spirit of our mind.

As I said earlier in the book, whatever has your attention has you. If you fill your mind with the good Word of God all day, the result will be faith instead of fear. Faith comes by hearing and hearing by the Word, but fear comes by hearing and hearing by the world!

Philippians 4:6-9 says, "Be anxious for nothing, but in everything by prayer and supplication, with thanksgiving, let your requests be made known to God; 7 and the

peace of God, which surpasses all understanding, will guard your hearts and minds through Christ Jesus. [8] **Finally, brethren, whatever things are true, whatever things are noble, whatever things are just, whatever things are pure, whatever things are lovely, whatever things are of good report, if there is any virtue and if there is anything praiseworthy—meditate on these things.** [9] **The things which you learned and received and heard and saw in me, these do, and the God of peace will be with you."**

I love this passage because as we *choose* to be anxious for nothing and have a grateful heart in our prayer requests to the Lord, the *peace of God* guards our hearts and minds! In addition, as we *choose* to set our minds on and meditate on sanctified things, plus DO what we've learned, the *God of peace* is with us! Truly, when we have the *peace of God* guarding us and the *God of peace* with us - fear, worry, and anxiety have no place in us!

We can allow God's Word to build a fence of His peace in our heart and mind, or we can let the worries of this life stress our heart and mind and choke His Word. We can take on more than we were designed to carry, or we can cast our cares on Him for He cares for us as 1 Peter 5:7 says.

Not Every Thought Is From You

It is easy to become a slave to your thoughts and emotions if you do not recognize not every thought you have is coming from you. I have met so many people who have made poor life choices because they thought or felt something. The enemy has told them, "Well, you feel this way so you must *be* this way." Or "Well, you've had thoughts about that deviant behavior so that must be who you really are." Nothing could be further from the truth! Some thoughts and feelings are ours, some come from God's Spirit, but some come from the kingdom of darkness.

Because you know this, you can begin to cast certain thoughts down and take them captive rather than them taking you captive. Once you get your thoughts and feelings under the authority of God's Word, you will be amazed how wayward emotions fall, and truth will arise.

In 2 Corinthians 10:3-5 (ESV), Paul describes taking every thought captive like a Roman soldier would take a prisoner captive — with force and authority! Here is the passage:

For though we walk in the flesh, we are not waging war according to the flesh. 4 For the weapons of our warfare are not of the flesh but have divine power to destroy strongholds. 5 We destroy arguments and every lofty opinion raised against the knowledge of God, and take every thought captive to obey Christ.

This descriptive text is Paul admonishing us not to be wishy washy with the world and it's carnality. We must cast down their arguments with God's divine weapons such as the Spirit of truth, worship, prayer, scripture, community, confession, abiding, mediation, and intercession. Many of these will be highlighted in the next chapter.

Draw a line with the enemy and tell him you will not give place to any of his thoughts or arguments any longer. Tell him no more fear, worry, torment, stress, or anxiety is going to live in you because Christ is living in you instead!

This is all part of gardening your heart because we cannot allow the soil of our heart to go unkempt! We must routinely and intentionally garden our heart with the truth of God's Word. Any good farmer will tell you if you just leave a field to itself and never cultivate it, something may grow there, but it won't be good!

Chapter Seven
Ensuring Your Worry Free Life

No, I am not offering you a money back guarantee, but I am offering you ten spiritual disciplines that I believe will help you bear fruit and walk out your obedience to a worry free life! I believe these are some "weapons of warfare" Paul talks about in 2 Corinthians 10:4-5 that possess divine power to tear down strongholds.

1. Are you abiding?

In other words, are you living connected to Jesus daily? In John 15:4-5 Jesus promises that if we abide (live, remain, stay) in Him we will bear much fruit. Here are the verses:

"Abide in Me, and I in you. As the branch cannot bear fruit of itself, unless it abides in

the vine, neither can you, unless you abide in Me. ⁵ I am the vine, you are the branches. He who abides in Me, and I in him, bears much fruit; for *without Me* you can do nothing."

He actually hints at a definition of abiding by saying *"Without me,* you can do nothing." So what is abiding? It is simply *including* Jesus in every aspect of your day, doing nothing 'apart from Him,' and living in the reality of your connection to Him. As a branch receives from and lives connected to a vine for the duration of its life, Jesus invites us to live connected to Him all day everyday. If you are stuck in traffic, include Him. If you are getting ready to have a tough conversation with a loved one, include Him. If you are getting ready to make a business decision, include Him.

Simply put, as Proverbs 3:5-6 says, "Trust in the Lord with *all your heart,* lean not on your own understanding; ⁶ *In ALL your ways acknowledge Him..."* That is abiding!

Because branches *receive* in order to live and bear fruit, it's important we are mindful of *how* we receive. In Matthew 13:15, Jesus unveils our three primary modes of receiving: Our eyes, our ears, and our heart. Therefore, some great questions are: Who and what am I looking at? Who and what am I listening to? Who and what am I letting take root in my heart on a daily basis?

2. <u>Are you walking with spiritual family?</u>

Proverbs 11:14 says, "Where there is no counsel, the people fall; but in the multitude of counselors there is safety."

I have found in my 25 years of ministry and walking with God's people, that despite their best intentions to follow Christ and obey Him, having practical accountability and relationships which support our growth and obedience is *very needed*. What a tremendous blessing to have true friends, who will fight for your freedom, alongside you, on a daily basis.

You become like those you hang out with so hang out with people who speak truth to you, love you, and challenge you to higher heights.

Are you intentionally walking with people who follow Christ wholeheartedly?

Are you hanging out with people who are merely indifferent about Jesus?

Do you have great friends and spiritual family in your life who care about your obedience to Christ on a personal level?

If not, it is time to begin asking Jesus for them.

3. Are you sitting with the Bible *and* its Author?

2 Timothy 3:16-17 says, "All Scripture is given by inspiration of God, and is profitable for doctrine, for reproof, for correction, for instruction in righteousness, [17] that the man of God may be complete, thoroughly equipped for every good work."

Learning to sit with, eat, and actually digest Scripture is truly life giving compared to just checking "Bible reading" off your to-do list. When we sit with Jesus in Scripture, we invite Him to take the written word and make it a personal word specifically to us and our heart. A personal word from God is called a "rhema" word in the greek language which means, "A spoken word made by the living Voice that inbirths faith in the hearts of yielded believers." This is the epitome of Romans 10:17 which says, "Faith comes by hearing and hearing by the Word of God." The words God speaks to us personally carry the activating power of faith in them!

Nothing excites me more than to see a Christ follower who has struggled to hear God's voice be able to make clear contact with Him. Simply take the time to ask Jesus, "Lord, I know what this passage says on paper, but what would you like to say to me personally through it?" Then write down what you hear Him speak so you can begin building a library of the Lord's living voice to you! If you are unsure if it's the Lord's voice you heard, ask a close friend who you know is a Christ follower and sits with Him regularly.

A personal rhema word from the Lord is so powerful because it initiates communication. Communication fosters relationship, relationship fosters intimacy, and intimacy fosters heart-felt obedience. Heart-felt obedience is the Lord's ultimate desire.

It is so important to personally invite Him into your time in Scripture as too many Christians read the Bible like it's a newspaper article or a history book.

In John 5:39-40 Jesus gives us a primary purpose of the Scriptures – to bring us to relationship with Him. Here is the passage:

"You search the Scriptures, for in them you think you have eternal life; and these are they which testify of Me. [40] But you are not willing to come to Me that you may have life."

Additionally, 2 Corinthians 3:6 also emphasizes the importance of *NOT* reading the Word apart from the Spirit of God and errantly trusting your carnal intellect to interpret it for you.

2 Corinthians 3:6 says, "…For the letter kills but the Spirit gives life (to the letter)."

You need a blessed balance of the Spirit and the Word! More important than just reading the Bible is reading it in the presence of the Author!

4. <u>Are you agreeing with your true identity?</u>

Who is your source for truth? Who is your source for your value, esteem, and identity? There are no greater questions for you and the Lord to sit together and discuss!

Luke 3:21-23 says, "When all the people were baptized, it came to pass that Jesus also was baptized; and while He prayed, the heaven was opened. [22] And the Holy Spirit descended in bodily form like a dove upon Him, and a voice came from heaven which said, "<u>You are My beloved Son; in You I am well pleased</u>." [23] Now Jesus Himself began His ministry at about thirty years of age..."

It never ceases to amaze me how God tells Jesus who He is (His Son), how greatly loved He is (His beloved), and that He has great value (He is well pleasing) *before* Jesus even began His ministry! Jesus has not performed one miracle or preached any truth to this point, yet His Father knows how important it is for Jesus to be secure in His sonship and His identity. He wants Jesus doing all those upcoming miracles and ministry FROM His Father's love and not FOR it!

In the same way, God desires you to take time each day to settle yourself in His sonship. The truest thing about you is what God says about you! It is not what others say about you, or how you feel, or even how you think of yourself. There is truth that exists beyond what you think, feel, believe, or even how you behave! Does that shock you?

<u>Have you ever considered that people's behaviors and actions may not be revealing what is true about them but rather that they've believed a lie and are simply acting out of that lie?</u>

1 Peter 1:23 says, "Having been born again, not of corruptible seed but incorruptible, through the word of God which lives and abides forever."

What this means is, if you're a born again child of God, the devil can't make you bad, he can only make you *think* you're bad! God made you who you are as a new creation! God birthed you with an internal seed in your spirit that CANNOT be corrupted!

Your born again spirit man has never been tainted with, much less overcome by fear, so doesn't it benefit you to identify yourself with your spirit man not your feelings? Your spirit man not your past? Your spirit man not others opinions? Who you are in your spirit is the *True You*!

I meet many people who are afraid one day God will expose them for who they really are. I pray He does! Because who you really are in Christ is a righteous, holy, faith-filled, love-empowered, fear-defeating child of God! Stop seeing yourself as a worrier and identify yourself as a mighty warrior in Christ! Know and believe the truest thing about you is who God says you are!

5. Are you staying immersed in truth?

In John 8:31-32 Jesus says, "If you abide in My word, you are My disciples indeed. ³² And you shall know the truth, and the truth shall make you free."

Again, is God's truth in front of your eyes, your ears, and in your heart daily?

If your answer is, "Yes, I go to church so I'm totally covered." I have news for you. No preacher/pastor is your Moses, mediating between you and God. You need your own relationship with the Lord first hand, not just input from somebody else's relationship. Sermons are not bad, but sermons as your only source for truth are bad. Living sermon to sermon instead of abiding with Jesus daily will not produce the fruit you desire to produce.

Listening to anointed messages via anointed messengers is good, it's just not enough. Thankfully, it is not "either/or" it's both – you can learn from Jesus personally *and* from others; so always be teachable and hungry to live in truth!

6. <u>Are you staying immersed in God's love?</u>

We have spent ample time in this book rediscovering, knowing, and believing the love God has for us. Of course, living an immersed life in God's perfect love that casts out all fear is a major key in you living an overcoming, worry-free life!

Ephesians 5:18 says, "And do not be drunk with wine, in which is dissipation; but be filled with the Spirit..."

Paul draws a correlation here between wine and the Holy Spirit because they are both influencing agents. When we are filled with the Holy Spirit, what is happening is that we are coming under the influence of the Holy Spirit within us. We are submitted to Him and begin allowing Him to coordinate our attitudes and actions!

One of the best ways to keep worry subdued is living immersed and full of the Spirit who's first fruit is love! God's love is such a force. His love is always there with us and in us so make a routine of practicing His loving Presence! Get into the habit of saying, "Father, I thank you for your love that drives out fear and that it is eternally present with me and in me. No matter what I face today, I am surrendered and surrounded by your steadfast love that keeps me unshakeable."

7. Are you walking with the Holy Spirit?

1 Corinthians 2:9-12 says, "But as it is written: "Eye has not seen, nor ear heard, nor have entered into the heart of man the things which God has prepared for those who love Him." [10] But God has revealed *them* to us through His Spirit. For the Spirit searches all things, yes, the deep things of God. [11] For what man knows the things of a man except the spirit of the man which is in him? Even so no one knows the things of God except the Spirit of God. [12] Now we have received, not the spirit of

the world, but the Spirit who is from God, that we might know the things that have been freely given to us by God."

What a stout passage. Paul is abundantly clear that just like no one knows all that is in a man except the spirit of that man, no one knows all that is in God except the Spirit of God! How amazing is it then that God would freely give us the gift of His Holy Spirit?!! He clearly did it for a couple of reasons. Yes, because He loves us, but also so that we can actually KNOW HIM! And not just know Him, but know *all things* that have been freely given to us by Him!

Verse 11 says, "No one knows the *things of God* except the Spirit of God." The Bible is clearly a 'thing of God' so who really can understand it but the Spirit of God? Righteousness is a thing of God so who can fathom it but the Spirit of God? Grace is in a word *amazing*, so who can grasp it and clarify it to us but the Spirit of God? God and His Kingdom are Spirit so who understands all that they are together but the Spirit of God! Having begun your relationship with God by the Spirit then my friends, make sure you are walking daily with the Spirit!

8. Are you practicing obedience?

What is your daily mindset towards obedience? Is obedience a positive or negative word in your vocabulary? Keep in mind that obedience is not law it is love! After all, Jesus said, "If you love Me you will keep My commands." Remember though, your obedience comes through self surrender to His internal power and Spirit, it does not come from self effort. Obedience is a *reflection* of your intimacy with God not a *requirement* for it.

1 Samuel 15:22 (NLT) says, "What is more pleasing to the LORD: Your burnt offerings and sacrifices or your obedience to his voice? Listen! Obedience is better than sacrifice, and submission is better than offering the fat of rams."

This means the Lord would rather you obey Him than offer up some alternative or bargaining chip.

Religion stays satisfied with hearing the Word and never applying it or living it. Simply memorizing the Word though, or telling others what it says, won't anchor you to your identity in

Christ. Hearing the Word won't stabilize you like when you act on it.

James 1:22-24 says, "But be doers of the word, and not hearers only, deceiving yourselves. [23] For if anyone is a hearer of the word and not a doer, he is like a man observing his natural face in a mirror; [24] for he observes himself, goes away, and immediately forgets what kind of man he was."

When we do not obey the Lord, we can forget our true identity and what kind of man or woman of God we are. That is not a good place to be, so let's turn it around and realize when we are doers of the Word it keeps us reminded of and grounded in our true identity. Obedience begets more obedience!

9. Are you reminding yourself what your disobedience costs you?

Disobedience hinders your relationship with God on your end not His. It undeniably clouds our thoughts and produces emotions like shame and guilt. Scripture says sin *wars against your soul.* Those negative emotions of course do not mean God isn't with you or doesn't love you, but it does allow the enemy to interfere with your hearing and the closeness of your fellowship! Take note of what Jesus says in Matthew 7.

In Matthew 7:24-27 Jesus says, "<u>Therefore whoever hears these sayings of Mine, and does them, I will liken him to a wise man who built his house on the rock</u>: ²⁵ **and the rain descended, the floods came, and the winds blew and beat on that house; and it did not fall, for it was founded on the rock.** ²⁶ **"<u>But everyone who hears these sayings of Mine, and does not do them, will be like a foolish man who built his house on the sand</u>:** ²⁷ **and the rain descended, the floods came, and the winds blew and beat on that house; and it fell. And great was its fall."**

You can bet the Lord is hungry to build a strong foundation in you! He desires to strengthen you to the point that you live an unshakeable life despite the world around you being shaken.

He knows when we only *hear* His words and do not *act* on them in obedience, we become very susceptible to the three tests of life: Rain, floods, and winds!

10. Are you practicing your oneness with Jesus?

1 Corinthians 6:17 says, "But he who is joined to the Lord is one spirit with Him."

Galatians 2:20 says, "I have been crucified with Christ; it is no longer I who live, but Christ lives in me..."

Do you understand that when you walk into the grocery store Jesus walks in there in you? You are a walking talking arc of the Covenant! You house and carry the very Presence of God!

Colossians 1:27 says, "To them God willed to make known what are the riches of the glory of this mystery among the gentiles; which is Christ in you, the hope of glory."

While it is true God is everywhere and certainly present in Heaven and beyond, it is important to recognize the very presence of Christ within us.

Separation Theology is the faulty belief that God is way off in Heaven somewhere, and we are down here trying to do our very best for Him.

In reality, there is no way we can be like God apart from God so He had to put Himself within us. This is why Jesus Christ came. He first went to the cross and eradicated our sin. In that bold and loving act, Jesus cleansed God's original temple, us, so He could finish what His assignment actually was – put God's Spirit inside all those who would receive Him.

The idea we are separate from Christ leads us into self-striving and burnout. We live too much of our Christian lives in our own efforts to 'get close' to the Lord instead of living and loving from Him as our ever present, internal supply.

As a child of God, born of His Spirit, you no longer have to believe the lie that you are separate from Him and thereby can practice your oneness with Him daily.

The (Absolute) Worthlessness of Worry!

Chapter Eight
Navigating The Promises of God And
The Problems of Life

Late in 2020 I had a good friend, Pastor Lee
Armstrong, on my podcast. He began a dialogue
with me that was truly revolutionary and inspired
me to write this chapter. Even though he has
experienced great tragedy and loss in his life,
Pastor Lee began to share how he and his wife,
Ginger, have remained happy, content, and full of
faith. <u>They have learned how to balance the
promises of God and the problems of life.</u>

Grief and adversity are struggles for all of us. I
venture to say, if you are reading this book, you
have had your fair share of difficulties and
distresses and you desire to overcome them. My
prayer is that this chapter aids you in your
perspective and builds a pillar of faith in your
heart that God is eternally good and trustworthy.

Even though we have many passages in Scripture

that promise us abundant blessings and victorious living, there are many Scriptures that promise us adversity, trial, and tribulation as well.

Too many Christians today either believe God is causing all the pain and tragedy in their life, or they think if they believe in Jesus just right and never sin, they'll *never* have pain or tragedy. My friend Lee will tell you, "Both those perspectives are wrong."

In John 16:33 (NLT) Jesus says, "I have told you all this so that you may have peace in me. <u>In this world you will have many trials and sorrows.</u> But take heart, because I have overcome the world."

Clearly, Jesus is not promising all of us a life on easy street, but rather that He will be our peace no matter what we face in this natural fallen world. He reveals there will be struggle right alongside what we've been promised in the way of blessing, peace, and provision.

I will never forget the Lord saying to me at a time of sorrow in my life, "Steve, the question is not – Why is this happening?" The question is, "Who is going to get you through what is happening?"

And of course, the answer was HIM! I have reminded myself and countless others of this word from Jesus to me. *In Me*, He said, you'll have peace. People who have been in seasons of grief, sorrow, and loss can find a measure of hope because He has promised to be with them.

I think we often get too concerned with how adversity found us. Did we do something wrong? Did we make God mad? Did we make the devil mad? Bottom line is, our focus needs to be on the ONE who is with us in our time of struggle and pain, no matter how it originated. Even after all Job went through, what God offers him in the end is Himself.

Pastor Lee, who has known as much heartache and loss as anyone, will tell you, "You have to know that God is good and that He promises to be there when trials come your way." You cannot let your emotions or feelings determine truth for you because suffering, loss, and tragedy are accompanied by feelings of suffering, loss, and tragedy. It may not *feel* like God is there with you, but you must KNOW God is there, because that's what He has promised! God simply cannot lie.

Psalm 147:3 makes the point, "He heals the brokenhearted and binds up their wounds."

Psalm 34:18 (NIV) adds, "The Lord is near the brokenhearted and saves those who are crushed in spirit."

Scripture says that God is near the broken hearted, even though at the time all they seem to feel is pain. Know that He is not only near you but that He is present with healing for you.

Hebrews 4:16 (NLT) says, "So let us come boldly to the throne of our gracious God. There we will receive his mercy, and we will find grace to help us <u>when we need it most.</u>"

There is grace for you in your time of need. I can testify that people who I thought may not be able to overcome a tragic loss or great pain in their life, have absolutely been able to because of God's grace. How? God's grace shows up in our time of need! We don't understand it until we actually need it, but at just the right time we begin to experience His strength and personal touch.

What a promise! God's grace is present for you for whatever the need is and for whenever you

need Him most! More than you need the answer
as to why tragedy or heartache found you, you
need healing. You need grace. You need to hear
the Spirit of God say to your heart, "I am here. I
am your Answer."

Pastor Duane Sheriff always says, "God is not
guilty, God is faithful." What he means is when
you don't understand what is happening around
you, recognize God is not the One putting you
through torment, He's the One who will be with
you in it. Fix your attention on God and remind
yourself that He is good and trustable.

The Faith Chapter

Hebrews 11 lists all kinds of heroes of the faith.
Yet, many people forget (or choose not to see)
that Hebrews 11 includes in the list people who
suffered greatly and never saw what they had
been promised come into manifestation.

**Hebrews 11:37-40 (NIV) says, "They were put
to death by stoning; they were sawn in two;
they were killed by the sword. They went
about in sheepskins and goatskins, destitute,
persecuted and mistreated – [38] the world was
not worthy of them. They wandered in deserts**

and mountains, hiding in caves and holes in the ground. [39] These were all commended for their faith, yet none of them received what had been promised [40] since God had planned something better for us, so that only together with us would they be made perfect."

Each of these received a good report of faith even though they didn't receive the promise. Faith for them was like believing for water their whole life, never getting it, but standing and trusting in the goodness of God the whole time! That is, in essence, what some of these heroes of the faith did.

In John 20:29 Jesus says, "Thomas, because you have seen Me, you have believed. Blessed are those who have _not seen_ and still have believed."

I love this passage because Jesus is implying it is those who believe, even though they have not seen or received what they were believing for, that are truly blessed in His eyes! It is like worship. I've said so many times, "Anyone can worship God when everything looks great, but true worship and love for God is when you worship Him even though things aren't going the way you would desire them to."

He's God and I'm Not - What a Relief

Recently in Oklahoma we had a terrible ice storm. I became incredibly distraught over all the trees around my house losing limbs under the weight of the ice. I had planted several pine trees the last couple of years and so I was especially feeling burdened for them. I prayed and prayed for the freezing rain to stop, and then for the temperatures to go up. I tried everything I knew in talking to God: Taking authority, begging, declaring, but nothing was changing.

After a couple more days of listening to tree limbs crack all around my house, I sat in my pick up one morning totally downcast. I was in pure lamentation over all the broken tree limbs and the ultimate fear of my trees dying, so I asked God to *please* speak to me. I turned on some worship songs and hit the shuffle button just hoping God could somehow meet me where I was. Sure enough, the song that came on was by Kent Henry that started with this lyric: "You are my God yeah, and I will ever praise you. You are my God yeah, and I will ever seek your holy face."

I suddenly realized that it was time to stop

accusing God of doing a poor job managing the weather, and instead humble myself as His son and His servant. He is My God! All the weight I was feeling immediately left me as He said, "Steve, instead of sitting here lamenting the poor job you think I'm doing as God, why don't you partner with Me and let's start cleaning things up and preserving what you have." The Holy Spirit then reminded me of this passage:

Hebrews 10:35 says, "Therefore do not cast away your confidence, which has great reward."

When I was uncertain of God's goodness, when I sat almost blaming Him for what was happening, I had zero peace. I was at total unrest. The moment I decided He is God and I am not, and that I should partner with Him to make things better, all my heaviness was lifted!

I know trial and tragedy come in life, we are promised them; but if you want to be fulfilled and not weighed down with life's burdens, remind yourself how good God is. Begin to partner with Him looking for His redemptive hand to work all things for good!

Chapter Nine
Your Worry Free Life Is Inside You

<u>The worry free life you're looking for is inside you by the Holy Spirit, not outside you by the right set of circumstances.</u> Too often we think we will only be free of worry when all our circumstances line up the way we want.

Instead begin to recognize you have a living Vine inside of you that can source you all the peace, stability, tranquility, and contentment you need!

In John 16:33 Jesus says, "These things I have spoken to you, that <u>in Me you may have peace.</u> In the world you will have tribulation; but be of good cheer, I have overcome the world."

He does not say in the right set of circumstances you have peace, He says *"In Me,* you have peace." As long as there are people around, you're going to face problems and difficulties. As long as this fallen world is around, you're going to encounter adversity. So, you can quit asking God for a worry free life *outwardly*, He's already given you one *inwardly*. As was mentioned earlier in this book, Jesus Christ is alive and well on the inside of you. Tap into Him!

1 John 4:4 in the Steve Eden translation says, "You will never face anything outside of you greater than Who is inside of you!" Simply begin to choose each day where your perspective, your peace, and your power will come from.

People say, "Steve, I just can't find peace." I say, "Where are you looking?" They often share some version of, "Well, I guess I've been looking in my job, my spouse, my children, the economy, my finances, politics, music, friends, and/or sports teams." What is the answer? Jesus said, *"In Me, you have peace."*

In John 14:27 Jesus says, "Peace I leave with you, My peace I give to you; not as the world gives do I give to you. Let not your heart be troubled, neither let it be afraid."

Galatians 5:22 says, "The fruit of the Spirit is love, joy, peace…"

Romans 14:17 says, "For the kingdom of God is not a matter of eating and drinking, but of righteousness, peace and joy in the Holy Spirit…"

Our peace is a fruit of our walk with and abiding in the Spirit, not a fruit of perfect situations in the natural realm. You can stress yourself using prayer to create a right set of circumstances, or you can use prayer to align yourself with the Prince of Peace.

Instead of praying outside/in prayers, pray inside/out prayers! In other words, pray and release peace and faith *into* situations rather than asking God to fix every situation so you can feel peace. Instead of praying away all the storms in life, ask God to use you to bring His peace to stormy situations.

There's nothing touching you today in the way of worry that Christ hasn't given you the power to overcome. This is the confidence you have in Him, that you cannot be defeated by worry or fear or anxiety unless you consent to be!

Don't Cope With Worry, Conquer It!

I pray that within the content of this book you are able to find at least a handful of truths that inbirth faith in you and further your intimacy, growth, and maturity in Christ. I pray you find the courage and confidence in Him to not only face, but overcome, whatever adversities come your way! Do not simply cope with worry, *conquer* it!

Acclimate to God's Voice. Agree with who He says you are. Agree with the truth of your incorruptible, inward identity. Make time to practice the disciplines the Lord has spoken to you. Unpack the truths you've seen. Use the weapons the Holy Spirit has shared with you. Be steadfast, immovable, intentional, always abounding in the work of the Lord, knowing that your labor in Him is never in vain!

I leave you with several truths and perspectives that already exist within your spirit and the mind of Christ inside you! Read them, speak them, declare them, and agree with them!

Here's what your spirit man already knows:

Psalm 23:4 (TPT) - Lord, even when your path takes me through the valley of deepest darkness, fear will never conquer me, for you already have! You remain close to me and lead me through it all the way. Your authority is my strength and my peace. The comfort of your love takes away my fear. I'll never be lonely, for you are near.

Psalm 27:1-3 - The LORD is my light and my salvation; whom shall I fear? The LORD is the strength of my life; of whom shall I be afraid? ² When the wicked came against me to eat up my flesh, my enemies and foes, they stumbled and fell. ³ Though an army may encamp against me, my heart shall not fear; though war may rise against me, In this I will be confident.

2 Timothy 1:7 - For God has not given us a spirit of fear, but of power and of love and of a sound mind.

Isaiah 41:10 (AMPC) - Fear not [there is nothing to fear], for I am with you; do not look around you in terror and be dismayed, for I am your God. I will strengthen and harden you to difficulties, yes, I will help you; yes, I will hold you up and retain you with My [victorious] right hand of rightness and justice.

Psalm 34:4 - I sought the Lord, and He heard me, and delivered me from all my fears.

Psalm 46:1-2 (NLT) - God is our refuge and strength, always ready to help in times of trouble. 2 So we will not fear when earthquakes come and the mountains crumble into the sea.

Psalm 91:4-6 - He shall cover you with His feathers, and under His wings you shall take refuge; His truth shall be your shield and buckler. 5 You shall not be afraid of the terror by night, nor of the arrow that flies by day, 6 nor of the pestilence that walks in darkness, nor of the destruction that lays waste at noonday.

Matthew 10:29-31 (TPT) - You can buy two sparrows for only a copper coin, yet not even one sparrow falls from its nest without the knowledge of your Father. Aren't you worth much more to God than many sparrows? 30 Even the very hairs of your head are numbered. 31 So don't worry. For your Father cares deeply about even the smallest detail of your life.

Psalm 112:6-8 (TPT) - Their circumstances will never shake them and others will never forget their example. 7 They will not live in fear or dread of what may come, for their hearts are firm, ever secure in their faith. 8 Steady and strong, they will not be afraid, but will calmly face their every foe until they all go down in defeat.

All Scripture is the New King James Version unless otherwise indicated:

NIV - New International Version
KJV - King James Version
MSG - Message Bible
NASB - New American Standard
NLT - New Living Translation
TPT - The Passion Translation
ESV - English Standard Version
TLB - The Living Bible
AMPC - Amplified (Classic)

SOURCES:

ANXIETY AND DEPRESSION ASSOCIATION OF AMERICA

AMERICAN INSTITUTE OF STRESS

TO FIND OTHER BOOKS BY STEVE EDEN GO TO:
AMAZON.COM AND SEARCH "STEVE EDEN"

ABOUT THE AUTHOR

Steve Eden is the Founding and Senior Pastor of Grace Church in Choctaw, Oklahoma

Grace Church is a loving and Spirit-led church that began in his and Stacy's home in 1999. Steve's passion for truth, the Holy Spirit, the advancement of God's Kingdom, and the necessity of daily intimacy with Jesus helps him effectively communicate and teach from God's Word.

Steve has served the Lord in full time ministry for over 25 years and has written several books including: "The True You," "Origins," "Love Letters From God," and "Finding Freedom Through Forgiveness." He has a sincere desire to see all of mankind find the lasting fulfillment that comes from God's Spirit living intimately and triumphantly in and through the human heart. You'll often hear him say, "Man is too great a creation to be satisfied by anything but God!"

Made in the USA
Monee, IL
09 October 2023

44253965R00056